NORTHUMBERLAND
COUNTY LIBRARY
WITHD
FOR SALE

OLD SCREAMER

'Old Screamer', officially the S.S. *Benbow,* was shipping medical supplies to Mulanda. This, at least, was what the Captain and his son, Tim Allison, thought, and it wasn't until a storm smashed open one of their crates of deck cargo that they discovered that they were smuggling arms instead.

Before they had time to telegraph the police, Lamorta and his friends, who were accompanying the cargo, had the whole crew at gunpoint.

How Tim and the other crew members manage to escape from this desperate situation makes *Old Screamer* continuously exciting as it moves towards the dramatic naval battle which marks the climax of the story.

Robert Bateman

OLD SCREAMER

ILLUSTRATED BY JAMES HUNT

HUTCHINSON JUNIOR BOOKS

HUTCHINSON JUNIOR BOOKS LTD
178–202 Great Portland Street, London W1

London Melbourne Sydney
Auckland Johannesburg Cape Town
and agencies throughout the world

First published 1970

This book has been set in Baskerville type, printed in Great Britain on antique wove paper by Anchor Press, and bound by Wm. Brendon, both of Tiptree, Essex

ISBN 0 09 102780 2

I

The ladder swayed, and Tim did the old trick—hooked both wrists round the handrails to hang on without spilling the mugs of cocoa he was carrying. The whole ship vibrated as a wave slammed into the starboard quarter, forcing up a jet of spray which blew back into Tim's face, drenching him. Then the cheerful rumble of the engine changed to an angry protesting clank as Old Screamer lifted her stern, and the propeller raced free of the water.

For a moment the ship steadied, and he took his chance to struggle up the last few rungs of the ladder to the chartroom. The sliding door was opened from the inside, and the mugs were grabbed from his fingers just as Old Screamer lurched into another deep roll.

Tim braced himself against the chartroom bulkhead. 'Dad, can't we run for the coast?'

Even Tim could not hear a word of what he said. He reached behind him and closed the door, shutting out some of the howling of the wind. 'Dad, won't she shift her deck cargo if she goes on like this? Can't we head for Bilbao?' Tim Allison looked anxiously at his father. He could tell that the same thought was going through both their minds—that Old Screamer, officially the S.S. *Benbow*, would take just so much of this before her leaky plates opened up and she sank.

Captain Bill Allison bent over the chart, and beckoned Tim to join him. 'Here's where we are.' He pointed to a pencil dot. 'We're too far south and west. In fact we hardly went into the Bay of Biscay at all. If we head for port it ought to be Vigo.' He stopped, and looked up, with a grin on his face. 'But we're not going to, Tim!'

'Why not, Dad? Why risk the ship?'

'Because there's a bonus for every day we save, and we need the money. Those big crates of Red Cross supplies are needed pretty badly by the rebels in Mulanda. There's an extra hundred pounds for every day we save in getting 'em there! Here, drink your cocoa, and then nip down and get the Mate to take over the bridge. I think I'd better check up on that deck cargo myself.'

Tim gulped his cocoa. He didn't look at his father, nor at the mountainous seas that crashed over the bows and across the crates on the fore deck. He was listening—for the dreaded sound he had heard only once in his fourteen years, the sound which had given the ship her nickname.

The sound from deep down in the heart of the S.S. *Benbow*—the scream of rivets tearing loose!

He opened the chartroom door and worked himself out on to the wing of the bridge. One moment he was staring down into the water, the next moment Old Screamer had rolled on her other beam, so that he was looking up into a wet grey sky across which raced deep clouds as dark as the churning smoke from Old Screamer's rusty funnel. He swung round, and looked astern at the water sluicing across the aft well deck, the twin lifeboats snug in their chocks beside the engine-room skylights, and at the grubby flag of Morenia which streamed out across the poop.

He had to admit it—the S.S. *Benbow* was a game old ship. And that flag told the whole story. Only ships like the *Benbow* flew that flag. Ships too old and worn out to be registered as British any longer, the world's tired tramps became Morenian. The shipping authorities in Morenia asked no questions—as long as the registration fees were paid. Nobody in Morenia cared if a ship was held together by nothing more than a coat of paint on top of the rust.

Tim waited for the ship to steady herself between waves, then darted down the two ladders to the main deck. A foot of water was frothing round the midships hatch and pounding against the base of the solid wooden door leading into the saloon and the cabins. Tim clung to the ladder, two rungs up from the deck, watching for a safe moment to leap for the door.

Bad timing would mean another surging wave while the door was open, and that would allow a foot of sea water to burst down the companionway into every cabin. He swung round on the ladder, and thumped with his fist on the thick glass of the steward's porthole.

A white face showed behind the glass.

Tim jerked his thumb towards the door.

A moment later it was opened—cautiously at first, then flung wide for him to jump inside. He heard the roar of the water thundering back across the deck as he slammed it shut again behind him. 'Thanks,' he shouted, and clambered along the narrow companionway to the First Mate's cabin.

The door was open. Big Rory McGuinness was wedged between the bunk and the washbasin, trimming the mass of red beard round his chin. 'Skipper wants you up top, Mr McGuinness,' Tim called out.

Rory raised a bushy eyebrow. 'What's up? I'll no' be a minute. She hasna sprung a leak, has she?'

Tim grinned at him, and shook his head. 'No, but my dad wants to check the deck cargo.'

Behind him, the door of one of the two passenger cabins opened suddenly. Tim turned round.

'The deck cargo? Did you say there is some troubles now with the deck cargo?'

'No, Mr Lamorta.' Tim looked at the round moon-face, and hoped he'd guessed right. He was pretty sure he had. This one was Lamorta, and the tall dark one was Gaspard, The third, the one he had never seen because he lay in his bunk all the

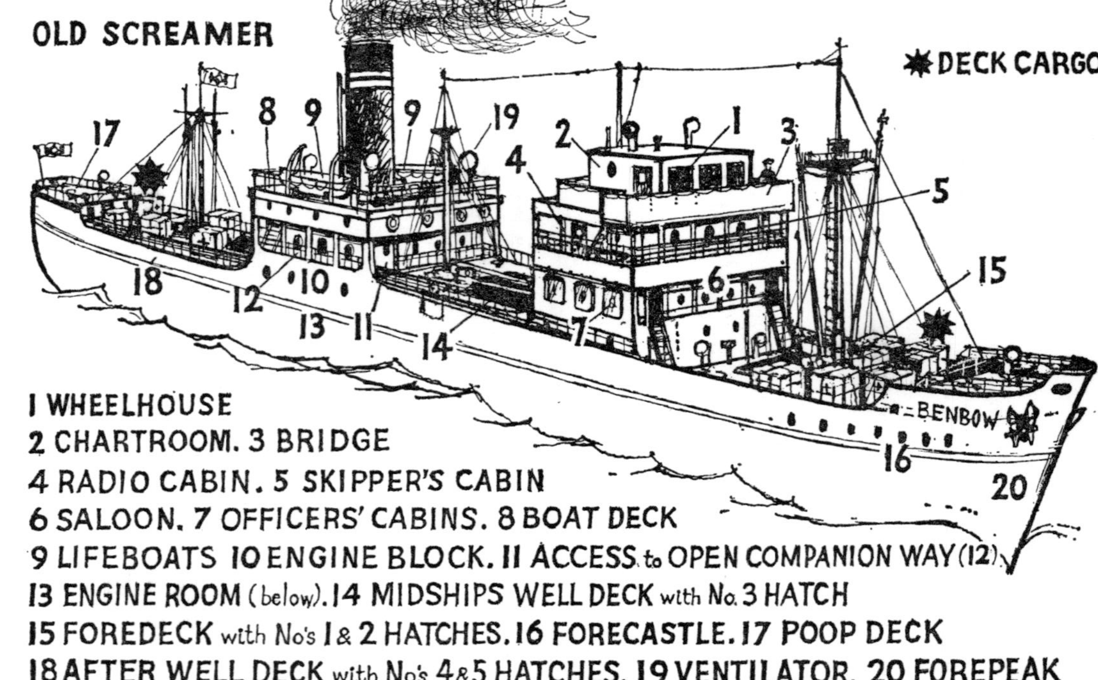

1 WHEELHOUSE
2 CHARTROOM. 3 BRIDGE
4 RADIO CABIN. 5 SKIPPER'S CABIN
6 SALOON. 7 OFFICERS' CABINS. 8 BOAT DECK
9 LIFEBOATS 10 ENGINE BLOCK. 11 ACCESS to OPEN COMPANION WAY (12)
13 ENGINE ROOM (below). 14 MIDSHIPS WELL DECK with No. 3 HATCH
15 FOREDECK with No's 1 & 2 HATCHES. 16 FORECASTLE. 17 POOP DECK
18 AFTER WELL DECK with No's 4 & 5 HATCHES. 19 VENTILATOR. 20 FOREPEAK

time, seasick, would be Charnot. 'No, nothing's wrong. But we always check deck cargo in a gale.'

'That is well. Be certain. Be very certain. You must understand, these medicines are of great importance. In Mulanda many peoples are dying because no medicines.'

'We understand, Mr Lamorta.' Rory McGuinness was speaking over Tim's shoulder. 'We'll no' lose your Red Cross boxes over the side. They're lashed down wi' . . .'

A tremendous crash cut him off in mid-sentence.

Tim swung round, staring at Rory McGuinness, then he raced along the companionway and flung open the door to the deck. Three feet of water surged in, toppling him backwards until his fingers caught the handrail and gave him support. He heard Rory shout, 'Hold on!' then the water slid away as Old Screamer's bows rose for the next wave. Tim hauled himself out on deck, with Rory right behind him. 'It sounded like one of the crates,' Tim yelled.

'Aye, one of the big ones away aft. Stay where you are, Tim, while I take a look.'

'I'm coming with you.'

White foam swirled angrily round them at knee-height. 'It's risky, Tim. Best stay where you are.'

But Tim was already working his way to the rail on the lee side, away from the incoming seas. Together they struggled along it, coming to a halt and bracing themselves each time a wave raced across the hatch coaming to hit them full in the chest with such force it knocked the breath out of their bodies. Tim glanced up to the bridge, and saw his father waving them back to safety. He turned away hurriedly, remembering Nelson, who too had failed to see the signal—when he didn't want to see it!

They reached the open companionway flanking the engine-room block.

Here, water was racing like the current of a fast river, its force nearly tearing loose their grip of the rail. Tim found himself seized by the waist and pulled round in front of Rory McGuinness, so that though he took the full force of the water, the Mate's body prevented him from being swept away. He saw a face at a porthole, and a hand waved towards the door leading to the engineers' cabins, but Rory pointed dead ahead, towards the well deck.

They could see it now, in front of them.

It was a sight that put a sick sensation of fear into Tim's stomach. There were dozens of massive Red Cross crates lashed to the deck. The gaps between them had turned into canals through which poured raging torrents of water.

Old Screamer heeled over on to her beam ends, and they clung on grimly to the rail above the well deck as hundreds of tons of water beat down on it, hammering on the tops of the crates. Tim saw the lashings of the crates become slack, then taut again. He pointed, and shouted to Rory McGuinness. 'Look—the crates are shifting!'

'Aye,' grunted the Mate. Water streamed down

his face. 'We'll need to get the bos'un to put the men on to tightening yon lashings.'

Something cracked, as sharply as the lash of a whip.

'Get down!' the Mate yelled, and they flung themselves to the deck behind the rail as over their heads flew the jagged end of the steel cable which had lashed down one of the crates. Tim had a horrible glimpse of twenty frayed strands of sharp wire as the cable flew past only two feet away from him.

And then, as they climbed to their feet again, Old Screamer went into another deep roll. Helpless, they watched the Red Cross crate burst loose from its one remaining cable and swing sideways, then crash into the hatch covering Number Four hold. The timbers cracked and buckled.

Old Screamer rolled back again, on to her other beam. The crate skidded across the deck into the rails, bending them outwards.

Then, on the next roll, it raced back once more to the hatch, slamming into it with a force that shook the deck under their feet. Broken timbers flew into the air, and the whole side of the crate caved in. Dark blue metallic objects about three feet long tumbled out and slithered across the deck.

Tim stared at them. They didn't look like Red Cross supplies.

And then, at the same moment, he and the Mate realised what they were. Both spoke at once.

'Guns!'

2

Tim looked at Rory McGuinness.

The same thought was racing through both their minds.

'Shall you tell him, or shall I?' Rory asked.

Tim looked for'rard along the lurching deck, then down again at the guns slamming between the scuppers and the hatch as each sea hit them. 'I'll tell him, Mr McGuinness.'

As he started back the way he had come, Tim could see his father up on the wing of the bridge. He seemed a long way away. The overhang of the boat deck beside the engine-room block boomed and echoed with the pounding of the seas as he groped his way from stanchion to stanchion through the fierce onrush of water.

Then, as he reached the open deck amidships, he halted, staring in horror as he watched Old Screamer's bows begin to rise up the flanks of the biggest wave he had ever seen. From beneath his feet he could feel the gallant thumping of the weary old engine thrusting with all its force to drive the ship onwards and upwards to safety, balanced on the crest of the wave.

But he knew, grimly, that she wasn't going to make it!

Too little power, too much deadweight—and too big a sea!

The upward journey of the bows came to a halt.

For what was probably two seconds, but seemed to Tim like a lifetime, the S.S. *Benbow* hung at a steep angle supported by the oncoming force of the wave.

Then she slipped forward, and he saw the crest of the wave appear, high and menacing, twenty feet above the bows.

Dimly he was aware of his father on the wing of the bridge, frantically waving a warning to him, but it was a warning he did not need. He thrust both arms behind the bulkhead rail, settled the rail in the crook of his elbows, then leaned back against the bulkhead with his face turned sideways. He filled his lungs with air, and closed his eyes.

For a few seconds there was a calm so deceptive that he almost opened them again. But years at sea had taught him that big waves do not go away.

You cannot flatten them out by wishing, or make them change direction by hoping. You brace yourself and endure them.

Even though he was prepared for it, and could hear the terrible booming rumble of it as it moved along the deck, when the wave hit him its force was unbelievably greater than he had expected. A hundred tons of water strikes more like a solid than a liquid; it stunned him, and the tremendous pressure against his chest drove all the breath out of his body.

Buried under a mountain of icy water, he fought against the instinct to try to breathe. With empty lungs, the need set in almost immediately, with the threat of unconsciousness only seconds away.

The last few steps were agonising. Though torrents of water were draining out of his clothes, they were still a dead weight, and his legs felt limp and rubbery with exhaustion. But he knew he had only a few seconds to reach safety, before Old Screamer met the next wave. Looking up, he could see his father at the top of the bridge ladder urging him onwards, but unable to help. Not until Tim reached the last three steps of the ladder could his father stretch down a helping hand to drag him to the top.

'Are you all right, Tim?'

Tim opened his mouth, but found he could not speak. He nodded his head.

'Better get below and change into some dry clothes,' said Captain Allison.

Only then did Tim remember the reason for his hurried dash to the bridge. He pointed astern, to where he could see Rory McGuinness braced against the rail overlooking the after well deck.

'Yes, I know, Tim.' His father quickly opened the wheelhouse door and pushed Tim inside. 'Get back against the bulkhead. Here comes another one. Not as big, but we're safer in here.'

Tim managed to clear his throat, and found he could speak again. 'One of the crates has broken loose.'

'I saw the top of it shift from up here. It can't be helped. But are the lashings still secure on the others?'

'It's not that, Dad,' Tim said. He glanced at the helmsman, then caught his father by the sleeve, and led him into the chartroom behind the wheelhouse. He closed the door securely.

'Dad, d'you know what's *in* those crates?'

Tim looked at his father. For one awful second he wondered if perhaps his father *did* know! Just how desperate were they for money? Could it have reached a point at which his father might have agreed to smuggle guns to the rebels in Mulanda?

But the thought went as soon as it came. That was one thing of which he could be certain: Captain Bill Allison would never do anything to help men kill each other.

He repeated his question.

'Of course I know, Tim. So do you. They're packed with Red Cross supplies.'

'Dad, you're wrong. They're full of guns.'

Tim saw the look of disbelief come on to his father's face. 'Tim, you must be dreaming! Those crates . . .'

'If I'm dreaming, Dad, then Mr McGuinness is, too! When that crate broke open, guns streamed out all over the deck.'

They both clung to the edge of the chartroom table as Old Screamer climbed sluggishly up the flank of another wave, and hung on its crest before dropping heavily into the trough beyond.

'What kind of guns, Tim? Rifles?'

'Automatic rifles, I think. Sten guns and so on. All hand stuff, as far as I could see.' Tim looked at the pool of water which had formed where he was standing. 'I didn't really stop to look.'

Captain Allison went back through the wheelhouse to the wing of the bridge. For a few moments he stared grimly across the fore deck at the raging seas beyond. Then he turned. 'Tim, there's only one thing to be done! Go back there to Mr McGuinness, and heave all those guns over the side. I want them all out of the way in ten minutes.'

Tim stared at his father. 'But, Dad, there are six-foot seas coming across that well deck! And the crate's knocked away the rail on one side.'

'Don't worry about that, Tim. You won't get swept overboard. We're changing course for Vigo.' He turned to the wheelhouse door and opened it a few inches. 'Take her round to east by south. Easy, now! We don't want to wake up our passengers.'

'Do you think they know?' Tim asked his father.

'Know what?'

'That the crates are full of guns.'

'I reckon they must.' Captain Allison looked at Tim again, right in the eyes. 'What I don't want them to find out is that *we* know. So get along aft and join Mr McGuinness.'

Even before he reached the deck amidships, Tim was conscious of the change of course. The swing of more than 150° meant that instead of battering her way through the enormous oncoming seas the S.S. *Benbow* was now running before them. Her speed was almost doubled, and no longer were the decks deep in water.

Rory McGuinness was down in the well deck checking the lashings on the remainder of the crates. 'I see the Old Man's changed course,' he greeted Tim.

'We're running for Vigo. Captain's compliments, Mr McGuinness, and he'd like us to throw all this lot over the side before the passengers see them.'

It took less time than they had expected. The sea had already swept some of the guns overboard; the remainder took only five minutes to dispose of. Then, with the well deck clear of water, they were able to get rid of the broken lashings and the remains of the smashed crate.

Rory McGuinness climbed back from the well deck. 'Aye!' he muttered thoughtfully. 'We'll be right enough so long as yon three gun-runners dinna find out what we've done.' He turned his head and looked amidships. 'Charnot's all right. He's flat on his back, seasick. But I'm no' so sure about Gaspard and Lamorta. Eh, Tim? If you were smuggling guns, wouldn't you come out every so often for a wee look to see all was well?'

'We'll be at Vigo by tonight. Then . . . well, I

suppose we hand them over to the Spanish police?'

Even with the ship on its new course they still had to work their way for'rard hand over hand along the bulkhead rail. The S.S. *Benbow* would remain steady on an even keel for ten seconds or more, then begin to shudder as she rose on the following sea, and finally the stern would drop back into the trough. But at least there was no longer any danger. A few more rivets must have sheared somewhere down below during those terrible moments when Old Screamer lived up to her nickname, but the pumps would deal with any leaks. They had done so often before.

Tim and Rory McGuinness passed the galley door just as Joe Redditch, the cook's assistant, risked opening it. Tim grinned at him. 'What's for lunch?'

'Stew.'

Tim made a face.

'You can count yourself lucky there *is* any lunch, after what we've been through in here!' Joe said hotly. 'The pans were sliding all over the stove.'

'What's to follow?'

'Tinned fruit. There was a hot pudding but it went on the deck. What's happened? Have we changed course?'

Tim looked uneasily at Rory McGuinness.

The Mate saved the situation. 'You talk too much, Joe! You'll have Cookie on your tail if you don't get back inside.'

Tim stood back to let Rory go up the bridge ladder ahead of him.

Captain Allison stood at the top. 'Well, Mr McGuinness?'

'All tidied away, sir.' The Mate laughed. 'In fact yon passengers would have to look a wee bit craftily even to see there's a crate missing.' He paused. 'What do we do? Arrest them?'

Tim's father shook his head. 'Let the Spanish police do that. They'll be quick off the mark once we reach Vigo. Tim, nip down to the radio cabin and tell Sparks to call up to arrange for police to come out in the pilot boat. Tell them we'll be off the port in six hours.'

'Aye, aye, sir.'

The radio cabin was immediately below the chartroom, down the ladder on the other wing of the bridge. Tim went through the wheelhouse. The short ladder led down beside a small jolly-boat protected by canvas: on the other side the radio cabin door was open.

Tim stepped inside.

'Get back, Tim!' the Radio Officer yelled at him. 'Can't you see there's . . .'

He was sitting at the radio desk.

Behind him stood Lamorta, with an automatic rifle jabbing into his ribs.

And as Tim stood rooted to the spot, a gun barrel was suddenly pressed into his own back. 'Get inside!' said a voice from behind him. 'Keep your mouth shut if you want to stay alive!'

3

For a moment Tim did not move.

Then the gun barrel prodded him forward into the radio cabin, so violently that he stumbled and went crashing into the Radio Officer. 'Sorry, Sparks!'

The gun barrel was thrust even harder into his back. 'Didn't I warn you to be quiet?'

He saw now who was behind him. It was the tall dark man called Gaspard.

Lamorta suddenly swung the barrel of his gun towards the radio transmitter and prodded at the glass dial of one of the instruments, shattering it. He pushed the barrel in further.

The Radio Officer jumped forward in his chair. 'Hey, what are you doing? You're wrecking my . . .'

His voice died away. He watched with horror as the moon-faced Lamorta moved the gun barrel from side to side. From inside the radio cabinet came more sounds of breaking glass, and wires drawn tight parted with a snap.

Only when it was quite plain that the radio transmitter would be useless without a major repair did Lamorta remove the barrel of his gun. 'Stay where you are!' he warned the Radio Officer.

Gaspard pushed Tim to the far side of the cabin. With the gun still raised menacingly, he backed towards the door, holding it wide for Lamorta to step past. 'Do as you are told, and you will come to no harm,' he grated. 'We shall see that food is brought.'

Then the door closed, and the key turned in the lock.

Immediately the Radio Officer jumped up from his chair and began hammering with his fists on the bulkhead.

'You're wasting your time, Mr Cafferty,' Tim told him. 'With the gale that's blowing out there, nobody can hear you.' He leaned over the radio desk and looked at the transmitter. 'Can you fix it?'

Cafferty was very young to be a Radio Officer—about twenty. He looked doubtfully at the transmitter, then burst out, 'Why did they do it?'

Tim told him.

'Guns?' the Radio Officer gasped. 'But how did they get them loaded aboard without anybody being suspicious?'

Tim shrugged his shoulders. 'Bribery, I reckon. A few hundred pounds given to the right people so that nobody asked any questions.'

Cafferty was now busy with a screwdriver, unfastening the front panel of the transmitter. He stopped suddenly as there came a rattle of machine-gun fire from out on deck 'What's that?'

Tim felt an icy chill down his back.

He could well imagine what it was. The next place the gun-runners would have made for would be the bridge, to take over the ship and turn her back on course for Mulanda.

He could not imagine his father letting that happen without a fight!

Tim looked at the porthole, wondering whether it would be possible to open it and wriggle out. He looked through it, at the open expanse of the amidships hatch twenty feet below. Even if he could just force his body through, what were the chances of being able to drop twenty feet without breaking a leg?

The Radio Officer, who was sitting in front of the transmitter examining broken parts, put down his screwdriver and came to join him. What Tim was looking at was Charnot, the gun-runner who had been seasick. With an automatic rifle in his hands

he was urging six of the crew along the wet deck towards the bows.

'They must be locking them up in the forecastle,' Cafferty said.

'But they can't run the ship themselves! Not with only three of them,.'

'They can for a while, Tim. And when they're stuck, all they have to do is let out a couple of men and stick guns in their ribs.'

'But what about the engine?'

'One man with a gun can keep the firemen stoking the boilers.' Cafferty had gone back to his radio transmitter, and was frowning grimly at the mess inside. 'I've got spares for some of these parts, but the rest I'll have to botch.'

'How long will it take?'

'Don't be daft, Tim! It could take an hour, or a week, or it may even be impossible. It's no use guessing. Another thing—they'll be back with food. They said so. I'll have to fix everything so they won't know I'm trying to repair the set.'

'I can warn you!' Tim jerked his thumb towards the porthole. 'I'll be able to see them coming out of the galley.' He unscrewed the dogs fastening the porthole, so that he could open it and have a wider view.

At that moment the S.S. *Benbow* changed course again. He saw the stern swing round sharply, and immediately a heavy sea caught the ship on her flank, heaving her over on to her beam ends. Tim hung on to the frame of the porthole with all the strength in his arms. Behind him there was a crash as Cafferty's chair went over, flinging him violently

against the door, and from below there was the crash of breaking crockery in the steward's pantry. Somewhere out on deck a voice cried out in pain.

The wave broke across the rail amidships, and swept across the hatch. Above the engine room, on the boat deck, a wall of water tore the starboard lifeboat off its davits and flung it against a ventilator. The boat rose high in the air, balanced on its stern, then rolled over with a gaping hole in one side.

Shuddering, the ship began to right herself as she continued the 180° turn to starboard. The sea cascaded off the boat deck, carrying the lifeboat with it.

Cafferty was lying on the floor, groaning.

Tim picked up the chair, then tried to lift the Radio Officer, but Cafferty was only semi-conscious, and almost a dead weight.

'Sparks! Wake up. Are you all right?'

Cafferty opened his eyes. He rubbed the back of his head. 'Whatever happened?'

'She rolled,' Tim said briefly. 'They've turned her to head south again. Sparks, you've just *got* to make that radio work, so we can call for help.'

Cafferty staggered to his feet. 'I'll do what I can. But I can't work miracles.'

Below the porthole, heavy boots echoed along the iron deck. Tim dashed back to his vantage point, just in time to see Rory McGuinness pushed into the passageway leading to his cabin. He could see the look of fury on the Mate's face—but also the gun Lamorta held just behind him.

Tim felt a sudden relief. If Rory was still alive, perhaps that meant that his father was safe too? The burst of gunfire on the bridge might have been only a warning.

'Tim, come and get hold of this wire while I use the soldering iron.'

'Can I risk it? What happens if I miss seeing them come up the ladder with the food?'

Cafferty shrugged his shoulders. 'It's a risk we just have to take. I can't do this job alone—not with the old tub heaving about all over the place.'

For the next hour Tim took turns between holding wires for Cafferty's soldering iron, and keeping watch at the porthole. On deck all was quiet, except for the occasional heavy sea pounding over the bows and sweeping aft in a flurry of white foam.

The cabin clock was at four-thirty when he gave the alarm. The galley door opened, and Joe Redditch came out with a loaded tray covered by a cloth. Behind him was Charnot, with a gun under his arm.

Joe staggered for'rard towards the cabin block, moving carefully in six inches of swirling water.

'They're coming, Sparks! I don't know if this is for us, but it might be.'

Hurriedly Cafferty hid the soldering iron, thrust a mass of wires back into the set, and screwed the front plate into place. He finished just in time to roll into his bunk as the key rattled in the lock.

Lamorta came in, and held the door open wide for Joe Redditch. He stared at Cafferty. 'What is wrong with the Radio Officer? Why has he gone to bed?'

'He hurt himself when the ship rolled.'

'Yes, it was very bad. I am sorry. Here is food for both of you.'

Tim looked at Joe Redditch as the tray was put down on the radio desk. He moved himself to stand between Lamorta and a half-repaired condenser which Cafferty had forgotten to hide.

Joe's eyes moved round slowly towards the porthole.

For a moment Tim did not understand.

And then he realised that Joe had thought of the same idea—that the porthole was big enough for him to be able to squeeze his way through.

And then what? Crash down on to the hatch top? Glancing first to see if Lamorta was watching, he shook his head.

Then Joe did a curious thing. He looked again at the porthole, and placed his finger on his cheek, pulling one eye open very wide.

'Hurry up, boy!' Lamorta ordered sharply.

Joe finished unloading the tray and went to the door.

'Is my father all right?' Tim managed to ask.

'He is on the bridge,' said Lamorta. 'My friend

Mr Gaspard is there with him. Providing he does as he is told, he will come to no harm. That applies to all of you.'

From the bunk, Cafferty burst out suddenly, 'But why d'you want to take guns to Mulanda? It just means the war will go on even longer and more people will get killed.'

'Why?' Lamorta halted in the doorway. Then he laughed. 'I am not interested in Mulanda, Mr Radio Officer. I am not concerned about who lives and dies—there, or anywhere else. My reason is a much simpler one.'

'What is that?'

Lamorta had stepped outside, and half closed the door. He put his head back inside for a brief, one-word reply to Cafferty's question.

'Money!'

4

'What did Joe mean?' Tim asked.

He had told Cafferty about the curious signal the cook's assistant had given.

The Radio Officer shrugged his shoulders. 'Why would anybody do that with his eye?'

'Unless . . . unless perhaps he meant I was to keep a sharp eye open at the porthole? Perhaps the rest of them have planned something?'

Cafferty hung on tightly to the sides of the bunk as Old Screamer rose on a wave and then dropped down what seemed like a sheer cliff on the other side. He changed the subject. 'What kind of rats are gun-runners who do it for money?'

Tim handed him a plate of thick corned-beef sandwiches and an apple. 'Hungry?'

Cafferty shook his head. 'Not really. I'll save it for later.' He rolled out of his bunk and went back to the radio desk. 'It should be safe for a while now.'

Tim munched a sandwich, leaning against the

bulkhead so that he could see out of the porthole. Down below, the Second Mate, Pat Lovery, was marched at gunpoint from the cabin block and across the deck to the bridge ladder. Tim wondered if this meant that his father would be allowed down.

Then he saw Joe Redditch again. The cook's assistant and three of the crew came out of the galley, arguing with the moon-faced gun-runner Lamorta. Joe was speaking angrily, ignoring the gun muzzle jammed into his ribs.

Finally Lamorta appeared to give way. He shepherded them along the deck towards the forecastle.

Five minutes later they reappeared, carrying blankets and mattresses. Tim pulled his head inside the porthole a split second before Lamorta looked up.

'What's going on?' Cafferty asked him.

'I wish I knew. Come and have a look.' He moved aside to let the Radio Officer study the scene.

Cafferty snorted. 'It's nothing. Their bedding got wet in the gale, that's all. The amidships hatch is the safest place to dry it. Look, they're putting up a line for the blankets. And they're spreading out the mattresses on the hatch top. See for yourself.'

Tim looked down cautiously. Joe and the Bo'sun

were doing just as Cafferty had said—right underneath the porthole.

And as Tim stared down, Joe glanced up!

Quickly Tim moved back from the porthole. 'I've got it, Sparks! D'you know what those mattresses are for? They're to break the fall if I go out of the porthole.'

Cafferty was back in his chair in front of the radio desk. He jumped to his feet. 'You can't risk it! You'd break your neck.'

'They're thick mattresses, Sparks. And they're white, so I shan't miss them after dark.'

Cafferty stared at him. 'You really do mean to do it, don't you?' He frowned. 'Okay, so you manage it without injuring yourself. What then?'

'In the darkness the ship's like a rabbit warren. Three men can't keep a watch on every corner of it.' Ideas raced through Tim's brain. 'I can let everybody out. They must have opened another crate to get the guns. That means I can bring out enough for all thirty of us.'

'If you don't get caught.' Cafferty frowned. 'I don't think I ought to let you try this. If it goes wrong, and you're hurt, the skipper will put the blame on me.'

Tim looked at Cafferty's waistline, then at the

porthole. 'Okay, then,' he said confidently, 'do it yourself. You go instead of me.'

'I couldn't get through, and you know it.'

'That leaves me, doesn't it? And I can't do it without your help.' Tim went to the porthole, and studied the leaden grey sky. 'It'll be dark in an hour. We'll try it then.'

While Cafferty continued work on the radio transmitter, he stayed at his vantage point, gripping the brass rim of the porthole tightly each time as the S.S. *Benbow* rose on a wave and dropped down the far side. He saw Joe and the cook make several journeys with food from the galley to the forecastle, the cabin block, and the engineers' cabins below the boat deck—each time escorted by Gaspard.

Darkness took a long time coming, even though the sky was already so heavily overcast. Old Screamer seemed to have discovered the rhythm of the big seas at last; she was riding more easily, lifting her bows briskly so that the waves had no chance to break over her deck. Instead they foamed angrily past her flanks, gleaming phosphorescently, leaping occasionally to thrust jets upward through the scuppers, but unable to flood the decks.

Cafferty said suddenly, 'I've done it! At least I think I have.'

Tim turned swiftly. 'Are you going to try it out?'

Cafferty nodded. 'You bet I am.' He gave Tim a long look. 'I want a promise from you.'

'Unh? What kind of a promise?'

'That if it works, and I'm able to signal for help, you won't climb out of that porthole.'

Tim grinned at him. 'Oh, that's okay! You can have your promise. I'm not all *that* keen to jump twenty feet on to a couple of wet mattresses.'

The Radio Officer waved him back towards the porthole. 'Check up to see that nobody's coming, before I switch on.'

As soon as Tim gave the all clear, Cafferty moved the switch that gradually stepped up current to the transmitter. He leaned forward, studying the dials as they came to life.

'Is it okay?'

'So far—yes. But we shan't know until I try to send a signal.' He put his hand over the morse key, and took a deep breath. 'Here goes!'

The moment he pressed down the key there was a blinding flash from inside the transmitter. Cafferty reeled over backwards in his chair. Smoke billowed round the radio desk. From the floor, Cafferty's hand shot out and switched off the current.

The smoke drifted out of the porthole.

The Radio Officer struggled to his feet. 'I must have . . . I must have got the wiring wrong,' he gasped, white-faced. 'I'll have to start all over again.'

'By the time you've done it, those guns could be killing people in Mulanda,' Tim said quietly. 'It's almost dark. In another ten minutes I'm going through that porthole.'

Cafferty stared round the radio cabin desperately. 'Why not wait a while? Look, they're bound to come back—if only to bring us a cup of tea. If they find you're gone, they'll start searching before you have time to do anything useful. But if you wait, then you'll have the whole night before they discover you're missing.'

That made sense, Tim had to admit. He went back to his job of keeping watch through the porthole.

'Sparks!'

Cafferty looked up.

'They're coming again. Looks like more food.'

Hurriedly the Radio Officer cleared the desk. He took a book from a drawer and began to read it. Tim sat on the bunk.

Five minutes later the door was unlocked and Joe came in, escorted by Lamorta. He was only given time to dump the tray on the desk, then the gun prodded him in the back and made him turn and go out again. 'Good night,' Lamorta said unexpectedly, and closed the door.

Tim jumped to the porthole, but Cafferty waved him back. 'Hang on fifteen minutes until everything's quiet. Anyway, get some food in you first. If you don't, you'll be starving by morning.'

Again, what Cafferty said made sense. Reluctantly Tim sat down, feeling annoyed at every minute's delay. No matter how hard he tried, he could not drive out of his mind the worry about what was happening to his father, Rory McGuinness, and the others. He ate very little, not because of lack of hunger, but because he was scared that if he did eat a full meal he might be unable to fit through the narrow porthole. When he had finished he climbed up on to the washbasin below the porthole. Outside it was now pitch dark. All he could see below was the blurred outline of the mattresses.

He gripped the brass fastening dogs on each side of the porthole, and swung his legs up. 'Hold on to my shoulders,' he whispered to Cafferty. He waited until the Radio Officer was in position, then in one quick movement he bent his knees tightly, and pushed both feet out of the porthole. He wriggled, and turned his body over as he moved through the gap until the brass rim was pressing hard against his hips.

For a moment he thought he was going to be unable to thrust himself through. Then, by a slight sideways turn, he was able to push one hip past the rim. He drew in his stomach muscles, turned again, and the other hip followed.

He looked down into the blackness as he eased his shoulders through in the same way. He felt more scared than ever before in his life.

'Now!' he said urgently. 'Push!'

5

The drop was brief and terrifying, but it was nothing to the shock of the landing. Tim tried to take it like a cat, with his muscles relaxed, but even as he went over backwards, even before he hit the mattress with a crash that seemed to jar every bone in his body, he knew he was no cat.

No cat lay on its stomach, teeth clenched to keep from crying out with pain, and rubbed its back to ease the agony that felt like a broken spine.

Tim felt as if the ship rolled over completely. For a few moments—or an hour—or ten years—he must have lost consciousness. When he recovered, he heaved himself into a sitting position and looked up at the porthole from which he had jumped.

It seemed an immense distance above him. Cafferty's face was just visible in the circle of the porthole.

Tim waved. Then, as quietly as he could, he slid off the hatch-top and into the shelter of the starboard alleyway running beside the cabin block.

He halted. He found he was breathing fast, as though he had been running a race, and his heart was hammering. Beside him was Rory McGuinness's cabin, but the curtains were drawn across the porthole, and he did not dare risk trying to attract the Mate's attention, for he had no idea how close the gun-runners might be.

Tim inched his way for'rard again, in the hope that he might be luckier outside the Second Mate's cabin. Pat Lovery was an older man than Rory, and a heavy sleeper when off duty, but Tim could not imagine him sleeping now, with the ship taken over by armed men.

The porthole was open and the light was on, but Pat Lovery was not there. That meant he was on the bridge.

Was the Skipper there, too?

If so, his father had been on duty twelve hours at a stretch. Surely the gun-runners would have allowed him to go down to his cabin now?

From Tim's position in the starboard alleyway it was impossible to see up to the portholes on the deck above, but if he moved out into the open he would not be able to see without being seen—let alone climb the ladder.

He decided to work his way aft, towards the galley

and the small cabin in the corner of the engine-room block which Joe shared with the cook. To do this he had to skirt round the amidships hatch unseen from the bridge. He squatted down close to the deck, keeping his head low, and thankful for the dark jersey he was wearing over his white shirt. When he reached the corner of the hatch he paused, to size up the distance he had to cover. Thirty feet? No, more like fifty, and much of it fully exposed. If the men on the bridge were looking for'rard, he was safe.

If not . . .

He darted along beside the hatch towards the safety of the galley.

Even as his foot caught in the big metal cleat welded to the deck he knew what would happen. He fell flat, thumping down hard on the iron plates, which rang like a gong.

There was a yell from the bridge. 'Who is that? Stay where you are or I shoot.'

Tim jerked to his feet and flung himself sideways, round the far side of the hatch, as a burst of gunfire hit the deck where he had been lying. The din of bullets slamming against the metal plates was deafening. As he crouched below the level of the hatch another burst tore across the tarpaulin covering it. Tim's mouth was dry, and his stomach had curled into a tight knot of fear. For a moment he felt too petrified to move. Then he realised that in the pitch darkness the man on the bridge could not possibly see where he was.

He moved again, more slowly this time, and reached the shelter of the galley doorway, but there he was lit up for a second by the glow from the stove, and another burst of gunfire banged against the iron plating a few feet away from him. A bullet hit him violently in the heel of one shoe, numbing his foot so much that for a few moments he thought he had been injured.

He was out of the galley doorway before the burst of firing could move any closer, and two yards further on he was right beside the open porthole of Joe's cabin. There was angry shouting from inside it—the voices of Joe Redditch and the cook both yelling at the tops of their voices for the firing to stop.

'Joe, it's me!' Tim shouted hoarsely.

There was sudden silence from inside the cabin. Then Joe said, 'Are you all right?'

'A bullet in the heel of my shoe, that's all.' Tim felt for the lock on the door, hoping Lamorta and his men would have left the key there.

But there was no key.

'I can't let you out,' he said through the porthole.

Then, hearing footsteps coming swiftly down the ladder from the bridge, he raced along the alleyway beside the engine-room block. At the far end he had a choice between the ladder down to the crates on the well deck, or ten vertical rungs leading up to the boat deck.

There was only a split second in which to decide. The automatic rifle opened up again, and bullets hit the deck around his feet. He swung round out of the line of fire, and clutched at the first of the iron rungs.

The climb to the boat deck took only a few seconds, and the moment he had made it he realised his mistake, for the whole area was within range of the bridge. To keep him pinned down, all the gunman had to do was return to the bridge and rake the boat deck with a heavy burst of firing.

And then, to Tim's horror, out from behind a thick bank of cloud came the moon!

The boat deck became brilliantly lit, and he had to dive for cover behind one of the tall ventilators flanking the funnel.

From the bridge, a second automatic rifle opened up.

Tim found himself only feet away from a terrifying crossfire which tore a gaping hole in the side of the one remaining lifeboat. And a hole appeared in the ventilator right beside him, from a bullet which must have passed right through its thin plating. He dropped hastily from behind the ineffective shield, and squirmed his way across the deck to the shelter of the funnel.

Here he was in a patch of shadow, invisible from the bridge or from wherever the first gunman was now firing. The stream of bullets continued to rip away the flank of the lifeboat, but in between bursts Tim could now hear an angry argument taking place on the bridge—an argument in which he could recognise his father's voice. At least, then, the Skipper was still alive! Tim could imagine his father's towering fury—and how much worse it would be if only he knew who was the target for the gunfire!

The gun at the stern end of the boat deck chattered again, spitting bullets all around him, then stopped. He heard a curse, then footsteps rang out on the starboard ladder.

It could mean only one thing—the gunman had run out of ammunition. Tim realised that to move was his only chance to get away. Crouching again, keeping in line with the funnel so that it shielded him from the man on the bridge, he backed towards

the ladder on the port side, and after a swift glance to see that the deck below was empty, he clambered down it, and also down the next ladder into the well deck where the crates were lashed.

There were gaps between them, wide enough for him to move along. And once again he was back in darkness.

Slowly getting his breath back, he waited for the next attack. Old Screamer was still pitching heavily as she butted head on into the seas, and the wind carried shouts back from the bridge. But there was no more firing, and no searchers came to look for him.

Half an hour passed before he realised why!

Of course nobody had come—it was more sensible to wait for daylight. On a small tramp ship, once day broke every hiding place would be revealed.

Tim had been squatting on the deck, resting; now he hurriedly clambered to his feet. His watch showed him it was midnight. That meant he had barely six hours before dawn—six hours in which to show his escape had not been simply a wasted effort.

He clawed at the crates of guns with his bare hands, stupidly, as if he could wrench the long nails out of the wood.

Then common sense sent him further aft, to the

carpenter's workshop in search of a case opener.

The door was padlocked.

Once again he found his heart was hammering inside his chest.

Twelve-thirty! Five and a half hours to go!

At this rate he would still be hanging around the decks with nothing achieved when they came to find him.

Wild ideas raced through his mind—so wild that he discarded them immediately. One of the three gunmen must be on duty in the engine room; could he sneak down there in the semi-darkness and overpower him from behind? Or was there a chance that just one cabin door, somewhere, had been left with the key in the lock?

And then, quite suddenly, a plan came to him!

6

It all depended on a big baulk of scrap timber on the well deck. Tim had noticed it when with Rory McGuinness he was throwing the guns overboard. Was it still there, or had the rough seas taken it over the side?

In the darkness, with not a sound from amidships, he was able to risk moving about in the gaps between the crates without crouching, and without peering round every corner. He discovered the baulk of timber by falling over it.

The timber was a four-foot piece of five by three, so soggy with water that he had to drag it to the rail. He hoisted it on to the top rail, balanced it there very carefully, and took a deep breath.

It *had* to work!

What kind of a shout did a man make when swept overboard? A yell for help, surely—trailing away gradually as he hit the water?

But there had to be a good reason for falling overboard, otherwise Lamorta and the others would be suspicious. Tim realised he would have to wait until Old Screamer not only pitched, but rolled as well. He stood with the heavy baulk of timber balanced on the rail for ten minutes, long minutes during which the ship seemed steadier than at any time since they had left port. His arms ached with the strain of keeping the timber from going overboard too soon. Each wave was dead in line with the ship's course; she rode up on them smoothly and easily, with hardly a trace of a roll.

And then, suddenly, Tim saw what he wanted—a slight cross-sea, just enough on the flank to make Old Screamer roll. He waited until the rail dipped down towards the water, then opened his mouth and yelled.

'He . . . e . . . elp!'

At the same moment he let go of the baulk of timber, and watched it drop into the water, sending up a big phosphorescent splash in the moonlight. Then, as he heard shouts from the bridge, he ducked behind one of the crates.

Footsteps hurried along the iron decks.

'Can you see him?' one of the gun-runners called out. Tim thought it was Gaspard.

The man who answered was definitely Lamorta. 'I cannot see anything. It must have been the boy.

Perhaps we injured him, and he lost his balance when the ship rolled. The rails are missing where the crate broke loose.' There was a slight pause, then Lamorta said harshly, 'It was his own fault. If he had stayed in the radio cabin it would not have happened. At least it saves us the trouble of searching for him.'

'We should get back to the bridge,' said the other voice. 'It is not safe to leave the Captain up there unguarded.'

The footsteps retreated.

Tim let out a breath which he seemed to have been holding for hours. Then he crept out into a patch of moonlight, and took a scrap of paper and a pencil from his pocket. He wrote: 'Dear Joe, try to tell the Captain I'm alive and well. Try to get the carpenter to leave a case-opener outside his workshop tomorrow night. And if you can, drop me a parcel of food between the crates in the well deck. Yours. Tim.'

He climbed up to the alleyway beside the engine-room block, and keeping close to the bulkhead, slid along to Joe's porthole. It was open, and he could hear snores from inside. He wrapped a penny inside the scrap of paper to give it weight, and tossed it through the porthole on to the cabin floor.

Then he returned the way he had come. He moved smoothly and swiftly now; three hours on the run had taught him to get about like a cat, sure-footed in the darkness. When he climbed up again to the moonlit boat deck he went straight down on his stomach, wriggling silently across the iron plating to the gaping hole in the side of the lifeboat.

This was the only stage at which he had to expose himself to the bridge. He looked for'rard, but even in the moonlight it was impossible to tell whether anybody on the bridge was facing towards him.

It would be luck. Good luck—or bad luck.

He stood up swiftly, thrust his body through the hole in the lifeboat, grabbed a thwart with both hands, and heaved himself to safety in the dark, smelly space beneath the covering tarpaulin. The glowing hands of his watch showed it was two-thirty.

He slept.

What woke him was heat.

Suffocating heat under the tarpaulin—which could mean only one thing, that it was not only daylight, but the first sunshine since Old Screamer had left port. Sweat was streaming out of him at every pore, and his mouth was dry with thirst. He crawled into the bows of the lifeboat and dragged up the tarpaulin until he had a narrow slit through which he could see out into the brilliant sunshine. There was a lot of movement on the wing of the bridge. Rory McGuinness was using a sextant to chart the ship's position; behind him, with his gun cradled under one arm, was Lamorta. Gaspard was leaning on the rail beside him, with a gun muzzle slowly sweeping the deck, on which work was going on as if no threat existed. Charnot must be below, in the engine room.

Tim wriggled back from his observation point to

the big hole through which he had climbed into the lifeboat. He kept his face just inside the hole, where a faint breeze made it possible to breathe more easily.

By his watch it was eight-thirty. That meant the heat was only just beginning. Ahead, unless the weather changed, was at least nine hours of baking sunshine. He could imagine what it would be like at midday, with not a drop of water to replace the sweat that was streaming out of him.

He lay in the same position for an hour. By then his thirst was becoming unbearable. He crawled back to the bow of the lifeboat, in the faint hope that Gaspard might have moved away. But the gun-runner was still in the same position—one which commanded the whole of the boat deck. Tim knew he had no chance of leaving the lifeboat, finding water, and returning unobserved.

Then, with a gasp of relief, he remembered where he was, and that he had checked the lifeboat's water supplies himself only the day before the S.S. *Benbow* left port. Of course there was water—gallons of it, and food as well, in the stern locker.

Five minutes later he was gulping down warm, brackish water, and clawing corned beef out of a tin with his fingers. The salt beef made him thirstier, but he no longer needed to worry, for there was enough water in the tank to keep him going for a fortnight. He took a tin basin out of the locker and used some of the water to wash his face, which gave him a new lease of life with which to endure the next few hours.

And endurance was what he needed! Even with his face at the gap torn away by the bullets, the heat made every minute stretch out interminably. Twice he had to duck for cover hurriedly; the first time it was Lamorta, who came up to shout indistinct orders to men securing the lashings on the crates below. Then, half an hour later, Gaspard arrived and gave him an uneasy ten minutes by prowling around examining the damage done by the previous night's gunfire. Tim scrambled silently into the stern of the lifeboat and lay there holding his breath as the gun-runner actually put his head inside the hole.

But after that he was left in peace.

Midday came and went. He was drinking water in almost continuous sips now to compensate for the sweating. His clothes were stuck to him, wringing wet.

The sun, which he had watched climb into the sky, vanished over the top of the lifeboat. In the limited range of his vision all was quiet now; occasionally he heard footsteps across the iron deck amidships, but he saw nobody.

Tim ate again—this time a tin of tomatoes and some of the hard, almost tasteless lifeboat biscuits. His mind began to race ahead to the coming night. Would Joe Redditch be able to do as he had been asked? Everything depended on the case-opener. He tried hard to believe that there was a second chance—that Cafferty would be able to repair the radio and call for help—but he could not convince himself. The memory of the jumble of wires and broken components in the transmitter casing was still fresh in his mind. It needed not Cafferty but a genius to turn that back into a radio that worked.

Suddenly the sun was gone. As always when a ship headed towards the equator, sunrise and sunset became almost as if operated by a switch. Shadows streaked across the deck, and deepened; lights gleamed at portholes.

And at last he stopped sweating.

Even though he had drunk gallons of water to combat it, he felt weak. He stripped off all his clothes, dipped his shirt in water, and used it as a flannel, washing himself all over. Though his clammy clothes were unpleasant to put on, the wash had freshened him, and after eating again he crawled out of the hole on to the deck.

There was moonlight again, but not continuously. Clouds were scudding across the sky, and every few minutes they blanked off the moon, shrouding the ship long enough for him to jump from one hiding place to the next.

He reached the edge of the boat deck, and crouched low behind the ventilator which had proved such a poor shelter when the bullets were flying. Staring up at the moon, he watched the edge of a cloud begin to bite its way into the yellow circle. The deck grew darker.

And then for a few seconds the moon was completely obscured. He leaped for the ladder, and scrambled down it out of sight from the bridge.

7

Within a minute he would know!

Tim clambered down the ladder to the well deck, and zigzagged between the crates to the far side, and the door of the carpenter's workshop. The sea was calm, and there was scarcely a sound apart from the steady thump of the engines. The moonlight filtered into the narrow passages between the crates, giving him enough light to move about easily. It also gave him enough to spot the parcel of food left by Jim. His spirits rose the moment he saw it. At least Jim had received the message safely. And if he had managed half the instructions, there was no reason to suppose he would not have managed the other half as well.

There was a note with the parcel: 'Case-opener in paint can by workshop door.'

Tim left the parcel. After a day of eating his way through the stock of food in the lifeboat he was no longer hungry. He hurried onwards to the carpenter's shop.

The paint can was there. And in it was a case-opener. Tim grabbed it, and swung straight round to the nearest crate, ready to prise it open.

Then he stopped.

This needed thinking about. Up to now he had hardly considered anything beyond the moment of getting the case-opener. But what he did with it was vitally important.

On a still night, just how much noise would he make in breaking open a crate? Another sobering thought came to him—supposing the broken crate had been the only one with guns inside? Supposing all the rest had artillery shells, or aircraft bombs—or even the Red Cross supplies they were supposed to contain?

There was only one way to find out.

But he still hesitated. If he found guns, what came next? He could drop one through Rory McGuinness's porthole, and another into Pat Lovery's cabin; a third into Jim's. There might be portholes open along the line of engineers' cabins too. But guns weren't everything. There had to be a plan, otherwise there would simply be a battle in which the crew were as likely to get hurt as the gun-runners themselves.

The ideal man to work out a plan was Rory. But

Rory had no way of passing it on to the others. The only one who could do that was himself.

Tim sat down beside a crate, and began work with the case-opener.

What would be the morning routine? That was another important question. Tim guessed that men were let out of their cabins only when they were needed. That meant there was little or no chance of Joe Redditch and the two Mates being able to join forces. Instead, one of them—whoever was called first—would have to overpower the man who came to his cabin, take his keys, and lock him in, bound and gagged, while he released the others.

To arrange all that meant a series of notes, one for every cabin at which he was able to leave a gun.

But first he had to *find* guns!

A plank of wood gave, and Tim plunged his hand into the crate. He brought out something long and heavy, which he thought was probably a mortar shell. Quickly he replaced it, and pushed the plank of wood back into position before moving on to the next crate. He had to work much harder this time before he was able to find his way in; when he did it was equally disappointing. The contents were army uniforms and steel helmets.

Tim began to get worried. Each crate was taking

at least half an hour to check, and it was now nine-thirty. There were about twelve more crates lashed to the deck; it didn't take much mathematics to foresee what would happen.

He was just starting on his fifth crate when he heard a faint scuffling sound. He froze, flattening himself on the deck, and waited.

Nothing happened.

He remained where he was for five minutes. then straightened up, almost laughing out loud. The ship's cat, of course! Gun-runners or not, Old Mick wasn't likely to change his nightly prowl in search of rats.

But when the sound came again he knew it was no cat. It was the thump of a shoe on the ladder down to the well deck!

Tim grabbed the case-opener like a club. At the moment he was in a gap between crates that ran fore and aft; he slid into one that led from port to starboard, where he could not be seen by anyone approaching from for'rard. He held his breath, listening again, waiting for a repetition of the sound.

What he heard was the shuffling once again, followed suddenly and unexpectedly by an unmistakable hiccup, cut short, as whoever it was clapped a hand over his mouth to stifle the sound.

Cautiously Tim put his head round the next crate.

Six inches in front of him, Joe Redditch hiccuped again. 'Sorry,' he whispered. 'Can't help it.'

Tim let out a gasp of relief—one that was far louder than the hiccup. 'Try holding your breath. How did you get out, anyway?'

'Same way as you did, through a porthole. Only I'm not so skinny. It took Cookie ten minutes to shove me through, and it hurt. How's it going?'

'Not so good. Everything but guns so far. Here, you take a turn.'

'We'd just better be lucky,' Joe Redditch said grimly. 'I heard that swine Lamorta talking to your dad. We'll be off Mulanda in thirty-six hours.' Joe eased the case-opener between two planks and wrenched downwards, putting all his weight on the end of it for maximum leverage. There was a scream as nails were torn out of the wood, and he stopped abruptly, looking uneasily towards the bridge. 'Keep your fingers crossed,' he breathed as they waited to see if the noise had been heard.

But there was neither sight nor sound of any movement for'rard and after a minute or two Joe gave the case-opener another jerk downwards, which lifted the last nails out of the wood.

Tim reached a hand inside.

'What have you found?'

Tim looked at him triumphantly.

'Guns!'

But the triumph lasted only a few moments. To get at the guns a second plank had to be removed. It was stubborn, and it was not until both of them put their weight on the case-opener that the nails lifted, once again with a noise that seemed deafening.

This time it *was* heard. A light flashed on the wing of the bridge. 'Quick!' Tim said urgently, pushing a plank into Joe's hands, and thrusting the other roughly back into position. As Joe replaced the second plank, he grabbed the case-opener and scuttled for cover.

Footsteps rang along the iron deck beside the engineers' cabins. A torchlight flashed down the gaps between the crates. It lingered for a moment on the crate they had just opened, and Tim held his breath.

Then the light snapped off and the footsteps retreated again.

They crept out of hiding and returned to the crate. A few moments later Tim had an automatic rifle in his hands. Joe pulled out four more. 'Great!' he said. 'Now we're all set.'

'Except for one little thing. Where's the ammunition?'

'Oh, grief—I hadn't thought of that!' Joe reached deeper into the gap in the crate. 'It's guns, guns, all the way. Hey, where did the thugs get their ammo?'

'There were boxes of it in the same crate as the guns.'

'Then there ought to be in this one, too.' Joe used the case-opener again to remove another plank, but when he reached still further into the crate, all he brought out was the barrel of what Tim guessed was a mortar. He pushed it away, not caring any longer about the noise he made. The hole in the side of the crate was now so big that he put his head and shoulders inside, then thrust forward with both feet until nothing above the waist was visible. From the depths of the crate his voice rumbled and boomed, and there were heavy metallic noises as he heaved the contents about in his search for ammunition.

He came out empty-handed.

Tim looked anxiously at his watch. 'We've only an hour until daylight. We'd better try another crate.'

But though they tried two more, they still had no ammunition, and the sky was becoming ominously lighter in the east. Tim suddenly abandoned the search.

'What are we going to do?' Joe asked him. 'Wait until tonight?'

Tim shook his head. 'That's too late. By then we'll be too close to Mulanda. The rebels might send out a gunboat to meet us. Worse still—what would happen if we met the Mulanda navy? They'd shoot the lot of us for trying to smuggle guns.' He scratched his head. 'We've just got to do this *without* ammunition.'

'Huh?' Joe stared at him blankly.

'It has to be done by bluff!'

8

Tim wrote the notes on scraps of paper torn from Joe's pocket diary. They said simply: 'If you can use an empty gun to capture a man, bring him to the well deck.

Then in the last shreds of darkness, they crouched with a load of guns and crept beside the engine-room block to the cabin Joe shared with the cook. Joe wedged a note into the muzzle of a gun and dropped it through the porthole. Then they crouched even lower and risked the sprint across the expanse of open deck beside the amidships hatch. Tim caught a glimpse of men on the bridge; if they had turned, there would have been no hope of avoiding discovery.

In shelter again beside the Mate's cabin, they pushed a note into the muzzle of another gun and dropped it through the porthole straight on to the bunk. It must have hit Rory McGuinness; there was an angry shout as he woke up, but with the sun now almost on the brink of the horizon they did not dare to wait to speak to him. Instead, they moved on to Pat Lovery's porthole with the third gun.

'Quick—we've got to get back to the well deck!' Tim said urgently.

Joe pushed the gun through the porthole, and then looked at the open deck they had to cross.

And at that moment the rim of the sun burst over the horizon, flooding the deck with light.

'We can't!' Joe gasped. 'It'd be crazy to try to cross it now.'

Tim glanced for'rard, but he knew already that there was no hiding place. The narrow strip of deck flanking the cabins led only to the fore deck, in full view from the bridge. 'We've got to try!' he whispered. 'We can't stay here.' Even as he said it he could imagine what would happen. Unable to see whether anybody on the bridge was looking aft, they would have to take a chance. They could creep across, and hope to go undetected—but that would take time. The alternative was a sprint—impossible to do without enough noise to sound the alarm, but fast enough to make them a difficult target. He swallowed on a dry throat. 'How fast can you run?'

Joe's eyes bulged. 'You're not asking me to . . .?'

'I'm not asking,' Tim said abruptly. 'I'm telling. We go together, from a standing start so they won't hear any noise beforehand. Come on, waiting won't help.'

Joe took a deep breath. Then he looked out to sea, at the sunshine sparkling on the water. 'I don't like the idea of bullets in my back. But you're right.' He moved forward, to stand beside Tim.

'Ready?'

Joe nodded.

'Now!'

They shot out of the shelter of the cabin block like sprinters off their starting blocks, with fifty feet of open deck in front of them. Their shoes drummed on the iron plating.

The shout came when they were halfway across. Then a second later, bullets set the deck booming. Rust rose in a cloud round them as they panted into the shelter of the engine-room block, where the overhang of the boat deck shielded them from the gunfire from the bridge.

But the respite could only last a second or two; the length of time it would take for the gunman to scramble down the ladder and be able to get them in his sights again.

Joe made for the way up to the boat deck, but

Tim grabbed him by the shirt and waved him towards the ladder leading down to the well deck. 'Our guns are down there. And we can draw their fire.'

'Unh?'

'They must be running short of ammunition by now. Down there among the crates we can make them waste it.'

They were only just out of sight when a sharp burst of firing spattered along the deck they had left. Glass crashed as a bullet hit a closed porthole; Tim heard a bellow of fury from the Second Engineer.

Then they were among the crates, wriggling through the gaps to where they had left the two remaining guns.

They halted, panting, behind the crates at the far end of the well deck. Tim wiped the sweat off his face. 'All right?'

Joe nodded. 'One of those bullets parted my hair for me.' He rubbed the top of his head. 'It must have missed by a millimetre.'

Tim stuck his head out just far enough to see the engine-room block. Lamorta, the man with the moon face, was standing at the top of the ladder, with his gun cradled under one arm. He was turning slowly, his eyes searching the gaps between the crates. Tim jerked back out of sight, then reached down to the deck and picked up one of the steel helmets he had found when rummaging in the crates.

'What are you going to do?' Joe asked uneasily.

'Draw his fire, just like I said. Watch!' Tim swung back his arm, and lobbed the steel helmet down the gap between the crates.

It worked.

At the very first bump of the helmet on the deck, Lamorta fired half a clip of ammunition, spraying the whole of the well deck. But above the ear shattering noise of the gun came a high-pitched scream of panic, which continued when the firing had ended. 'Stop it, you idiot!' Gaspard's voice rang out. 'There are bombs in some of those crates. Do you want to kill us all?'

Beside Tim, Joe leaned over as though he was about to be sick.

Tim watched Lamorta lower the gun. There was a whispered conversation between the two men, then Gaspard went away, leaving Lamorta on guard at the top of the ladder. Even when Tim risked putting his head further out of shelter, Lamorta did not fire.

'D'you think the other fellow's gone to wake

Cookie?' Joe asked. 'What'll he say when he sees I'm not there?'

'Cookie won't give him a chance to say anything,' Tim said. 'Then he'll grab the keys and let everybody out.'

Joe gave a snort. 'It *sounds* easy enough. But don't forget Gaspard's gun is loaded. Cookie's is empty.'

'But Gaspard doesn't know that! The moment he opens the door he'll feel the cold muzzle of Cookie's gun in his ribs. Then all Cookie has to do is change guns.'

'I still say it sounds easier than it is. Cookie's never tried to hold up a man with a gun.'

'Cookie knows how close we're getting to Mulanda,' Tim said grimly. 'He'll do a good job.'

But when half an hour had gone by without anything happening his confidence began to ebb away.

'I told you,' Joe said. 'Cookie's made a hash of it.'

'What about Rory McGuinness, then? And Pat Lovery?'

'Maybe he hasn't been to their cabins yet. Cookie's the man he'd call early. We have to be up early otherwise nobody would have any breakfast.'

Tim looked again at Lamorta.

One thing was certain—the whole ship was still under the gun-runners' control, and heading due south towards the rebels' landing place in Mulanda. Something had to be done, and done fast.

The something was obvious, but sweat broke out all over Tim the moment he thought of it. He mopped his face with his sleeve. 'Come on,' he said. 'We're going to hold up Lamorta!'

Joe Redditch goggled at him. 'You and me? With empty guns?'

'He doesn't know, does he? The way he'll see it is this: we could fire upwards at him without any risk. But if he fired down at us he could do just what Gaspard warned him about—blow up the whole ship. All it needs is just one bullet in the wrong crate and the bombs would blow the whole stern off!' Before Joe could argue, he suddenly moved out from cover, with his gun pointed straight at the man on the top of the ladder.

'Lamorta!'

The gun-runner looked down at him, his round face tense and drawn. Then hurriedly he glanced round, as if to shout for help.

'Keep silent, Lamorta, and drop your gun. You're covered from two directions.' Tim hoped he was right; that Joe had taken up position. A moment later, from the look on Lamorta's face, he knew this was true.

Slowly Lamorta lowered his gun to the deck.

Tim came forward between the crates, keeping Lamorta covered. Halfway up the ladder he raised his gun to his shoulders, to keep the muzzle trained on its target.

A split second later, as Lamorta dived, he realised his mistake—that in raising the gun he had revealed there was no ammunition clip attached. Flinging

himself forward on the ladder he jabbed hard with the gun at Lamorta's ankles when the crook's hands were shooting down towards the loaded gun lying on the deck. There was a sharp crack of metal against bone, and Lamorta jerked backwards, yelping with pain as he grabbed at his ankle. A moment later he was lunging forward again—but by then Tim had the loaded gun, and was dropping the empty one into the well deck.

Joe came up the ladder at a run.

'Search him for keys,' Tim ordered.

Lamorta glared at them. 'You will regret this, boys. I will not let children interfere with my plans.'

'You can forget your plans,' Tim snapped. 'Gun-running's all over for you, Lamorta. Any keys, Joe?'

Joe Redditch shook his head.

'Who's got the keys, Lamorta?'

A slow smile appeared on the moon face. 'Find out! Two boys with one gun that is half-empty. That is no match for two determined men, each with a full gun.' He held out his hand 'Give me the gun, boys, then you shall go back to your cabins and we will forget this ever happened. I do not bear malice.'

'I do,' Tim said simply. 'I don't like being shot at. Joe, it can't be Charnot who has the keys, because he's below in the engine room.'

'Gaspard, then.'

'Exactly. We'll have to tie up this thug and gag him. See if there's anything on the engine-room grating.'

There was. On the top grating, high above the engine, out of sight from below, Joe found an old coil of lifeline used for safety along the decks in heavy weather. He tied Lamorta by the wrists and ankles.

'What about a gag.'

Joe looked ruefully at the sleeve of his shirt. 'My old mum's going to ask questions about this next time we're home,' he said, then ripped open the seam at the shoulder. He tied it tightly round Lamorta's head. 'Sorry if it hurts—but so do bullets.' Between them they carried Lamorta on to the grating above the engine, and secured him to the handrail.

Tim let out a deep breath he felt he'd been holding for hours. 'Now for Gaspard!'

'He'll be on the bridge. We can't shoot at him without the risk of hitting your dad or the helmsman.'

Tim considered that for a moment.

'We'll have to tempt him down.'

'How?' Joe glanced outside, and then led the way back on to the deck beside the engine-room block.

'One of us could start up a noise. He'd come down to investigate. Then the other one gets the gun in his ribs.'

'You're forgetting something. He can use his gun up here without any danger of blowing up the ship.'

Tim frowned. Then he glanced back towards the engine room. 'Maybe we should tackle Charnot first? Yes, why not? Joe, you'll have to get me Lamorta's jacket.'

'What's the idea?'

'I'm going to be Lamorta. And you're going to be an engineer I'm bringing down below to go on watch.'

Joe blinked. 'We'd never get away with that!'

'Charnot will only see us from below. He'll see the soles of our feet and the gun, and the jacket. Remember, he won't be expecting trouble.'

Lamorta made furious strangled sounds from behind the gag as they untied his wrists, removed his jacket, and replaced the rope again. When he saw what they were about to do he began struggling, and drumming his heels on the iron grating to attract the attention of Charnot thirty feet below in the depths of the engine room. If Old Screamer's engine had been new and quiet he might have succeeded, but the wheezing of leaky steam pipes and the heavy clank of worn bearings would have drowned even a shout.

Joe led the way down.

'Keep your head up,' Tim warned, jabbing him in the back with the muzzle of the gun. 'Don't let Charnot see your face.'

'Get that thing out of my backbone,' Joe grumbled, as he reached the foot of the first ladder and shuffled along a short grating to the next.

There was only another fifteen feet to go before they were face to face with Charnot. As he turned, Tim risked a hasty glance into the dimly lit space at the foot of the ladder.

Charnot was sitting on a bench, with his gun across his knees. He looked up sleepily. 'Is that you, Lamorta? Is everything well?'

Tim pushed Joe forward, so that he stumbled down the last ten steps of the ladder. It diverted Charnot's attention for a second. By the time he looked up again he was staring into the muzzle of Tim's gun. He made a convulsive move to grab his own gun from his lap—but the suddenness of it jerked the gun on to the deck.

'Get it, Joe! Stay where you are, Charnot.' Tim's heart was thumping painfully with a mixture of fear and excitement. 'Mr Rathbone, where are you?'

The Second Engineer walked round from the far side of the main engine. His jaw dropped open. 'Tim! We all thought you were dead. How did you . . .?'

'Have you a length of rope to tie him up?' Tim asked.

'Yes, I . . .' The Second Engineer was still staring goggle-eyed at Tim. He reached up and unhooked a length of oily rope from a hook, then looked at the sleeves of Charnot's clean white shirt. 'You'll be able to wash your shirt in gaol, Mr Charnot!' He tied Charnot's wrists, then secured the rope to the guard-rail round the electricity generator. He turned back to Tim. 'What happens next? There are two more of 'em up top.'

'One more,' Joe Redditch told him. 'We've got Lamorta already. Gaspard's the only one left.'

'The trouble with Gaspard is that he's on the bridge,' Tim said. 'My dad's up there with him. Once he finds out what's happened, all he has to do is stick a gun in my dad's ribs and threaten to shoot unless we give in.'

The Second Engineer frowned. 'I don't see any way round that.'

Tim sat down on a bench. 'What we need to do is get him down here somehow. If we . . .'

He stopped, as Charnot strained at the rope and let out a shout which echoed round the engine room. The Second Engineer reached into a bin and brought out a huge lump of greasy cotton waste. 'D'you want a gag, Mr Charnot? Because if you do, we can fix you up with one very easily.' He looked at the black grease on the cotton waste. 'It won't taste very nice, but if you insist . . .' He held it up, and moved nearer to the gun-runner.

Charnot went white. He backed towards the guard-rail. 'No! No, not that. I promise you I will not shout again.'

'You're wasting your breath, in any case,' Tim

told him. 'Gaspard can't hear you.' He swung back to the others. 'Supposing we call him on the voice-pipe and tell him Charnot is sick?'

Joe Redditch shook his head. 'He'd be suspicious. If Charnot was too sick to speak, Gaspard would guess we'd pinched his gun.'

'But Gaspard doesn't know anything! He thinks we're still in the well deck, with Lamorta on guard.'

'But if he came down, the moment he saw Lamorta wasn't there he'd start spraying the whole ship with bullets.'

Tim thought about that for a moment. 'Then we have to catch him before he reaches where Lamorta ought to be. Look, we've got two loaded guns. Mr Rathbone, you stay down here. Give us time to go up top, then call up the bridge.'

'What do I tell them?'

'Tell them . . . oh, say that Charnot's fainted. Seasick, or something. Sound as if you're scared—tell him it wasn't your fault.'

'I hope you know what you're doing,' said the Second Engineer. 'Has either of you ever fired a gun?'

Tim shook his head. 'I hope we don't have to. I don't want to kill anybody—not even Gaspard.' He began to climb the ladder. 'Come on, Joe. Give us five minutes, Mr Rathbone. Okay?'

At the top of the engine room, Lamorta was still where they had left him. His eyes flashed angrily and he mumbled through his gag as they passed.

'Can we reach the galley door without being seen from the bridge?' Tim asked Joe.

'I think so. It's a safe bet as long as Gaspard's on the far side.' Joe put his head out of doors. There was nobody in sight on deck. 'Shall we make a run for it?'

'No. Running's too noisy. Better take it quietly, and keep close to the bulkhead.'

They crept round the corner past the ladder where Lamorta had been stationed, then moved slowly along past the engineers' cabins. The sun was dazzlingly bright on the water; Tim had time to notice three ships hull down on the horizon, with black smoke pouring from their funnels.

'Wait!' Joe called a halt. 'This is as far as we can go if Gaspard's on the starboard wing of the bridge.'

Tim came to a sudden stop. 'Oh! That's something I hadn't thought of.'

'Unh?'

'I was reckoning that he'd automatically come along the starboard side, where we could get him as he comes past the galley door. But supposing he uses the port alleyway?' He paused, racking his brains for an answer, knowing that within a minute or so the Second Engineer would be calling the bridge through the voice-pipe. 'Go back, Joe!'

Joe looked bewildered. 'Go back where?'

'To the engine-room door. Hide in there. 'I'll go in the galley. Then if one doesn't catch him, the other will.'

Joe crept back the way he had come. Tim moved forward a few inches, to try to see the wing of the bridge.

Gaspard was there—on the starboard side, but looking for'rard. Could he risk the six paces to the open galley door?

He took a chance—sacrificing speed for silence. As he reached shelter he glanced up again just as Gaspard turned to his left and went into the wheel-house. That would be to answer the shrill whistle of the engine-room voice-pipe.

Tim's heart thumped as he waited.

One more minute would see it all over—either they would be in full control of the ship or they'd be running for their lives, with Gaspard's gun peppering the deck behind them.

Through the gap between the hinges of the open galley door he could see three rungs of the ladder leading down from the starboard side or the bridge.

If Gaspard came down on that side, there would be a moment's glimpse of his feet.

The wait seemed to last for hours. Was Gaspard arguing through the voice-pipe with the Second Engineer?

Even an argument would not have lasted as long as this. It was obvious that Gaspard had gone down the port side, and was now being held up by Joe Redditch.

Tim stepped out of the galley.

Straight on to the muzzle of Gaspard's gun!

9

Tim froze in his tracks, but what he really wanted to do was kick himself. He looked at the cold, hard glint in Gaspard's eyes—a glint that could mean only one thing.

So this was how it ended, then? Thirty-six hours of freedom, thirty-six hours of roasting in a stifling hot lifeboat, of being shot at, of working in a frenzy to find guns, and then finding ways of capturing Lamorta and Charnot—all of it ended this way, with a quick burst of fire from Gaspard's gun?

It seemed impossible. Being shot dead was something that happened in the night, or the grim grey light of dawn, not in cheerful blazing hot sunshine.

'You are a stupid child,' Gaspard said in a grating voice. 'Did you really think that I could be tricked so easily? I was not deceived by the message on the voice-pipe. This galley door was the only place you could be hiding—and so I came down the other ladder, so that you could not see me, and then I crossed the deck. Drop your gun, boy!'

Tim's lips were dry. He moistened them with his tongue. 'And if I don't?'

Gaspard shrugged his shoulders. 'It will make no difference. Unlike Charnot and Lamorta, I am not a merciful man. I do not mind who I kill. You are in my way, and you are a nuisance.' The gun jabbed harder into Tim's stomach.

Tim closed his eyes. Would it hurt? Or would there be so many bullets, so fast, that he would be dead before the pain could travel upwards through his body to his brain?

To his astonishment he *heard* the shooting, instead of feeling it. And instead of the sharp, high-pitched rattle of an automatic rifle it was a deep roar, followed by a dull explosion which sounded as if it was some distance away.

If he had died, it had been painless, and he didn't feel any different now it was over.

Slowly Tim opened his eyes again.

Gaspard was still in front of him, but the automatic rifle had been swung away. The gun-runner, grey-faced and shaking with fear, was staring towards

the horizon and the creaming bow-waves of three oncoming ships.

A flash of fire burst from one of them, followed by another roar and the scream of a warning shell passing overhead. In a sudden crazy move Gaspard raised his gun and fired a long burst at the oncoming ships, even though they were at least two miles away.

From the bridge Tim could hear shouting, and

then the sharp clatter of the steering engine as Old Screamer changed course.

Tim leaped for his own gun, swept it up from the deck with one hand, and pushed it into Gaspard's back. 'Drop it!' he yelled.

Gaspard let the gun fall. 'It is the Mulanda Navy! If they catch us, they will kill me and my men for trying to smuggle guns to the rebels.'

'If one of those shells hits the ship they'll kill *all* of us,' Tim pointed out. He kicked Gaspard's gun into the scuppers, then nudged Gaspard into the starboard alleyway of the cabin block. As he hoped, the bathroom was unlocked, with the key still in place. 'In you go!'

Gaspard looked at him pleadingly. 'But if you lock me in there, what happens if they sink the ship? I shall drown.'

'You'll drown anyway. We'll all drown. One lifeboat went in the gale, and you've shot the other one full of bullet holes. Give me all your keys.' He grabbed them, then slammed the door and locked it.

Then he raced to the bridge, just as a third shell skimmed overhead and hit the water two hundred yards beyond the ship.

His father was just outside the wheelhouse, with

binoculars raised to look at the three oncoming ships.

'Dad!'

Captain Allison lowered the binoculars for a moment. 'Good work, Tim! Quick, get Sparks out here to send a signal on the lamp.'

Tim dashed down to the radio room and unlocked it. He stared at Cafferty in amazement; even though thirty-six hours had gone by, the Radio Officer was still sitting at the desk, working on the wrecked transmitter. Tim beckoned him out on deck; he came out, blinking in the glare of the sun.

Old Screamer had now completed a 90° turn. To Tim's astonishment, though, she was not running from the three attackers, but heading straight towards them. As soon as he reached the bridge he grabbed his father by the shoulder, and pointed. 'Dad, we're . . .'

'Get Sparks to flash a message telling them to come alongside—that we've taken three gun-runners as prisoners.'

Cafferty braced himself against the bridge rail, and focussed the signal lamp towards the bridge of one of the oncoming ships.

'What are they, Dad?'

'Corvettes. Old wartime ones sold to the Mulanda

Navy by ours. Somebody must have tipped them off that we were gun-running.' Captain Allison's voice changed abruptly. 'Get your heads down!'

They heard the scream of the shell for a fraction of a second before it struck. The explosion, down on the boat deck, lifted the wreck of the one remaining lifeboat high in the air and tossed it on to the midships hatch. The funnel, almost cut through at its base, lurched drunkenly as if about to fall, then settled back into place.

'Their gunnery's none too good,' Tim's father said coolly. 'They ought to be hitting us with every shot at this range. Sparks, keep on sending that message.'

But Cafferty was staring helplessly at the remains of the signal lamp lying on the bridge, smashed by the force of the explosion which had torn it from his grasp.

'Flags, then,' Captain Allison called out. 'Hurry, man, hurry!'

Old Screamer and the Mulanda corvettes were now only a few hundred yards apart. Tim could see men working at the for'rard guns of all three ships. Flame burst from the muzzle of one of them, and the shell hit the water only a few feet from their bows.

There were muffled shouts from the men locked in the forecastle. 'Get them out, Tim,' Captain Allison ordered. 'Go round and get everyone out. Sparks, call down the voice-pipe and tell Mr Rathbone I want more speed—and more smoke.'

'More *smoke*?'

'That's what I said, Mr Cafferty. All the smoke the engineers can manage.' Captain Allison swung back to Tim. 'When you've got the crew out, go and release Mr McGuinness. Tell him I want every man on the boat deck.'

'Aye, aye, sir,' Tim said smartly, but with no idea what his father was driving at. There were no lifeboats, so how could it help to save lives by having every man out on the boat deck?

'Tell Mr McGuinness I want that funnel over the side. I don't care how he does it.'

Tim was now completely bewildered. 'Aye, aye, sir,' he said again, and started down the ladder.

By the time he reached the fore deck a machine gun had opened up aboard one of the oncoming corvettes, but the fore deck was flanked by steel plating instead of rails, and by ducking down as he ran he was safe from the stream of bullets bouncing harmlessly off it.

Suddenly Old Screamer was right between two of the ships, with a gap of no more than fifty feet on either side. Tim flung himself on the deck to escape a vicious crossfire which lasted about five seconds. He caught a glimpse of gunners frantically trying to bring their guns round to bear on the S.S. *Benbow* without the risk of firing point blank into their own ships.

As the corvettes streamed away, the firing died down. Tim scrambled to the locked doors of the forecastle. As soon as he opened it men streamed out, yelling and cursing.

'Make for the boat deck!' Tim shouted, then ran back to the cabin block to release Rory McGuinness.

The Scotsman was in an even greater fury than the crew. When Tim opened the cabin door the empty gun was jabbed into his ribs before the Mate realised who he was. Tim gabbled an explanation of what was happening, then followed with the Skipper's orders about the funnel.

McGuinness stared at him doubtfully. 'Are you sure you're no' imagining all that?'

'It's not imagination. Quick, Mr McGuinness!'

Tim raced back to the bridge as Old Screamer heeled sharply in a full-speed turn through 360°, one that brought the starboard rails under water and sent dishes clattering off the racks in the steward's pantry. Over his shoulder Tim saw the men on the boat deck grab wildly at the engine-room fanlight to avoid being swept overboard. The funnel swayed again, teetered on the brink of going over, and then hung precariously with wisps of smoke pouring out around the broken base.

He reached the bridge. His father was looking with satisfaction at the funnel, tilted like the Tower of Pisa. 'That shouldn't present Mr McGuinness with any great problem,' Captain Allison said calmly. The ship had now completed the turn. From below there was a frightening rumble and vibration as the ancient engines raced faster than they had done for many years. Ahead the three corvettes were swinging round to come back into the attack.

And then Captain Allison unhooked a megaphone from a stanchion. He put it to his lips, took a deep breath, and bellowed, 'Stand by to ram!'

10

'Grip the rail, son!'

Tim stared at his father.

'Go on, do as I say. Grip the rail. Now hang on tight. Helmsman, port a little. Easy does it.' Captain Allison's voice was as calm as if he were berthing Old Screamer back home on Tyneside. 'Stand by, helmsman, for a quick starboard turn. Hold it! Hold it until I give the order.'

A shell hit the poop, exploding with a force that almost flung them to the deck. Tim didn't dare look aft, for fear he'd find half the ship had vanished.

'Now! Hard a starboard!'

The steering engine clanked and clattered; Old Screamer's bow swung round, timed perfectly as one of the corvettes completed her turning circle. The thinly plated flank of the Mulanda ship, with huge rust patches showing in the grey paint, loomed up dead ahead. Tim saw frightened faces as men rushed from their guns.

And then with a shriek of tearing metal, the S.S.

Benbow's bow cut into the corvette, rolling her on her beam ends.

From amidships came another shriek of metal as the impact jarred Old Screamer's broken funnel. Slowly it leaned over on its side, then crashed on to the boat deck and rolled over into the water.

And then Tim understood his father's order to the engine-room. The thickest, blackest smoke he had ever seen came rolling up from the gaping hole, blotting out the whole ship from the amidships hatch to the poop in the first few seconds.

Captain Allison swung round to Tim. 'Get below and release Mr Lovery. Tell him to find the Bo'sun and check the forepeak for leaks.' He picked up the engine-room voice-pipe. 'Full astern, Mr Rathbone. Give her all you've got.'

The engines slowed, halted, then started up again. The screech of metal was repeated as the S.S. *Benbow*'s bows pulled clear of the damaged corvette, which rolled back from her beam ends, lying low in the water.

A stream of machine-gun fire shattered the windows of the wheelhouse.

'Are you all right, helmsman?' Tim heard his father shout, then he raced down the ladder again to the Second Mate's cabin.

Pat Lovery was pounding with his fists on the locked door. This time no explaining was needed; Lovery waved to the Bo'sun, who was coming down with the rest of the crew from the boat deck, and both hurried off to check the forepeak.

Tim decided to make his own check of the damage to the poop. He fought his way along through thick, choking clouds of smoke to the well deck, and paused between the crates, wishing there was time to search for a mortar and shells, so that he could have the satisfaction of firing something back at the enemy. But much more urgent than a mortar was the need to fight tongues of flame bursting out round the door of the carpenter's shop!

He rushed for a hose, then realised he had no way of signalling the engine room to start the pump. No way—except one.

Was the risk too great? Or would Lamorta have the sense to do as he was told.

Tim raced back across the well deck, up the ladder, and through the door to the top grating of the engine room. Lamorta, ashen-faced, was straining at his ropes. Tim untied them. 'Get down below and tell them to put full pressure on the fire hoses!'

Dazed, Lamorta nodded, and went down the ladder into the engine room. Tim turned to the hose, unwound it, and opened the valve.

The hose swelled suddenly, and a fierce jet of water almost flung him to the deck. He struggled to drag it towards the carpenter's shop, then found extra hands beside his own. Rory McGuinness, his face almost black with soot, grinned at him. Together they hauled at the hose, which kicked and bucketed with the strength of a huge serpent. Tim was soaked to the skin in the first few seconds, but it was welcome in the blast of heat that was coming from the poop.

Rory McGuinness managed to bring the jet under control and swing it right into the heart of the blaze. The door of the carpenter's shop, glowing bright red, had swung open; inside there was an inferno that hissed angrily as the deluge of water poured into it.

Tim was dimly aware that guns were still firing, but the dense cloud of smoke from the gaping hole on the boat deck where the funnel had been now blanked off all of the ship except the few feet around them. He could see nothing, only feel the whole ship shudder as shells exploded in the water alongside. Every few seconds the deck under his feet canted over steeply as up on the bridge his father ordered sharp changes of helm.

And then suddenly, only six feet from the rail, the grey flank of a corvette loomed up through the smoke. Tim saw dark faces staring at him in surprise, then the Mulanda seamen jumped to a machine gun on a swivel mount.

Rory McGuinness saw, too.

There was no shelter, only an open rail between them and the machine gun. No time to run across the hatch-top and drop down behind an inch of steel plating on the other side. And what would happen if a stream of bullets ripped into the crates on the deck?

Rory jerked at the hose, turning the jet through a 90° angle until it shot straight into the faces of the men at the machine gun.

Then the corvette was past, and he was able to twist the jet back into the blazing poop.

Tim pointed at a sudden channel of flame racing out across the deck.

Rory nodded. 'Paraffin!' He doused the new outbreak. 'Keep well back! It may blow up.'

He spoke just in time. Tim was aware, without hearing it, of a great orange ball of flame bursting out of the carpenter's shop on to the hatch-top, setting the tarpaulin alight in seconds. He saw Rory McGuinness's hair catch alight; he tore off his shirt, swung it through the jet of the hose, and slapped it down hard on the Mate's head.

The jet skimmed low over the tarpaulin, dousing the new blaze, then streamed back into what was left of the carpenter's shop. The flames were weaker now; like a beaten army they retreated. Rory handed the hose to Tim. 'Keep it covered! Don't let up until it's not even smouldering. Another explosion could set these crates alight.'

To play safe, Tim hosed down the sides of the crates nearest to the carpenter's shop. They were already so hot that steam gushed up as the water hit them. Then, inch by inch, he moved forward, driving the fire back, seeing the red glow fade to grey and the last tongues of flame flicker out.

Rory McGuinness had gone back to the bridge.

Tim looked at himself. Stripped to the waist, he was coated with a thick layer of wet, greasy soot that made him almost as dark as the Mulanda seamen on the corvettes. He found his shirt, and pulled it over his head as a protection against sparks as he climbed the ladder to the poop. The deck beneath his shoes was still so hot that it melted the rubber of his shoes; he hosed them, then drenched the few sections of the poop that were still dry.

He could still see nothing further away than the crates in the well deck. What was going on for'rard was a mystery. The only certainties were that the engines were still rumbling and throbbing at top speed, and that Old Screamer was laying over hard from one course to the other, to shake off the aim of the Mulanda gunners firing into the pall of smoke.

It was safe to take it for granted there was now only one corvette attacking them. Another must have stopped to pick up survivors from the vessel Old Screamer had rammed. Everything depended on how long they could twist and dodge in their cover of smoke without taking a direct hit from one of the corvette's shells.

Heaving and straining at the heavy hose, Tim managed to wedge the nozzle in a deck cleat so that the jet could be left to stream through the poop skylight into the smouldering shambles below. Then he climbed down on to the well deck, stepped across the tops of the crates, and searched in the choking pall of smoke for the ladder up to the alleyway beside the engineers' cabins.

He found it not by sight but by feel. As he groped his way up it a shell screamed low overhead, proving that the Mulanda gunners were still able to come to their target in spite of the smoke.

The alleyway was ankle deep in broken glass from portholes, and what looked like fragments of hatch boards and tarpaulins, but it was not until he reached the galley that he was able to see where they had come from. He stopped, and stared at the gaping hole where the midships hatch covering had been. On either side of the ship the rails were twisted, and the bulkhead of the cabin block had been dented by the force of the explosion. A shell must have exploded right in the centre of the hatch.

There was no longer a bridge ladder on his side of the deck; he picked his way across to the port side and began to climb.

Suddenly reaction set in; the strain of the past twenty-four hours caught up with him, and he had to cling tightly to the rails, fighting to stay conscious as the ship seemed to twist and turn in front of him.

'Tim!'

His father's voice came to him as if from a tremendous distance away, but it was enough to give him the strength and encouragement he needed. He swallowed hard on a dry throat, and began to climb again.

The canvas windbreaks along the bridge were in tatters, ripped by bullets. Broken glass from the wheelhouse windows littered the steps of the ladder. But at the top, Tim saw his father.

And the Skipper was laughing!

'I think we're going to make it, Tim!'

Tim reached the bridge, and looked round at the sparkling sea ahead and the haze of thick smoke astern. 'Where's the corvette, Dad?' he asked.

Captain Allison pointed. 'In there, somewhere. Two minutes ago we steamed right past her, heading south. That was when she fired that last shell. She'll go five miles south in all that smoke before she finds out we didn't go south after all. Then she's got to circle round and try east, west and north.' He went on into the wheelhouse, picked up the voice-pipe, and called out, 'All right down below, you can cut your smoke—but keep up your speed.' He stopped, and listened. His face grew serious. 'Is it bad?'

Rory McGuinness, coated in soot and sweat, came in from the other wing of the bridge. He, too, looked grim. 'Second Mate says we're badly holed in the bows, sir!'

Captain Allison nodded. 'Thank you, Mr McGuinness. I expected this. The S.S. *Benbow* wasn't built for ramming.' He turned back to the voice-pipe. 'Cut your speed, then. Give her whatever you think is safe.'

'Anything I can do, sir?' Tim asked his father.

'Yes, there is. Go down with Mr McGuinness. I want derricks rigged on the for'rard hatches—we're going to shift cargo.'

Tim saw the look of surprise on the Mate's face. 'Shift the cargo?'

'Yes, Mr Mate! As fast as you can—get it up out of the for'rard hatches and heave it over the side. I want the bows up high in the water. Then we've got a chance the bulkheads will hold.' Captain Allison paused a moment. 'Where are those three gun-runners?'

'They're all locked in the bathroom.'

'Then fetch 'em out. Give 'em the job of opening

up the hatches. Half an hour shifting hatchboards won't do 'em any harm.'

Tim was alert again now as he followed Rory McGuinness down the ladder and along the forecastle. Most of the crew were hurriedly dragging their suitcases out from under their bunks. The for'rard end of the forecastle was stove in; Tim could see daylight through the gaps in the plating. Six inches of water swilled around his feet. And from below there was an ominous rumble as tons of water thundered against the first of the bulkheads.

Rory waved the men to the winches, then signalled the bridge for steam pressure to be put into the deck-pipes. Almost immediately the pipes crackled and twanged as the pressure began to build up. Somebody tried a winch; the cable drum started to move, slowly at first, then gathering speed, lifting a derrick up to its hoisting position. On the hatch-top Gaspard, Lamorta and Charnot, their neat white suits now crumpled and sooty, were sweating as they lifted out the heavy baulks of timber to reveal the neatly stacked boxes underneath.

Tim joined four men loading the boxes. Winches rattled, and load after load splashed over the side.

'What's in them?' Tim gasped as Rory McGuinness came past.

'Machinery. It's no' guns—I've had a look. It's a pity to lose it all, but the insurance will cover.'

Pat Lovery came up from another inspection of what was going on below the forecastle. He looked anxious. 'There's water pouring in down there!' he shouted across the deck.

'How far down is the hole?' Rory McGuinness asked him.

'It's hard to tell. Maybe three feet below the water-line.'

Rory McGuinness raised his voice. 'Hear that, everybody? If we're to save the bulkheads, we've got to lift the bows three feet, and fast!'

The winches raced. Tim, on his loading team, was joined by Joe Redditch. Together they heaved crates which normally they'd have thought too heavy to lift. They worked in the blazing sunshine, knocking off in relays for a ten-minute break for lunch which the cook brought out of the smoky haze still enveloping all the stern half of the ship. Captain Allison's order had reduced the smoke, but the lack of a funnel meant that even now it was barely possible to see more than twenty feet.

By mid-afternoon they were standing on the 'tween decks, fifteen feet below the hatch-top, and Pat Lovery went down to inspect the bows again—

this time from the outside, on a rope ladder with a safety line round his waist. Swinging wildly on the end of the ladder, he shouted up, 'It's a tear about two feet long. I can see the top of it clearly every time she pitches.'

Rory McGuinness and Tim went back to the hatches. Number One hatch, with large boxes inside, was the easiest, for it took less time to make up each load and shackle it to the derricks. The boxes in Number Two had to be stacked in loads of twelve. Tim saw Gaspard, stripped to the waist now, working as hard as the crew. Charnot and Lamorta were sulking in a dark corner; Tim routed them out and they went back to work sullenly on the first boxes in the lower hold.

The sun went behind the clouds. Tim became aware uneasily that the wind and sea were rising. From below he could hear the sullen thump of tons of water hitting the bulkhead at the for'rard end of Number One hold each time Old Screamer dipped her bows into a wave.

Deep down in Number One hold somebody shouted. Rory McGuinness scrambled down the ladder hurriedly. 'What's the matter?'

'See for yourself, sir! Water's coming through.'

'That means the bulkhead's starting to give way,'

Rory shouted up to Pat Lovery. 'Mr Lovery, how big is the entry into the forepeak?'

'About four feet by three.'

'Could we heave some of these crates down there and break the force of the water?'

Lovery looked thoughtful. 'We could try. Tim, Joe, Bo'sun, bring a crate along and we'll see if it fits.' He waved to the men on the winch to drop the next load on deck. Tim and Joe seized one end of a crate; the Bosun, his shoulders straining with the effort, took the other single-handed. They staggered into the forepeak entry, and looked down the black hole in front of them. From below there was the sinister rumble of water against the bulkhead. A rivet snapped with a noise like a pistol shot.

The Bo'sun edged his way round the crate to join Tim and Joe. 'Ready, boys? Right, then. When I say push, give it all you've got.'

The crate slid forward into the gap.

And stuck!

'It's half an inch too wide,' the Bo'sun gasped.

Pat Lovery, beyond the hole, examined it carefully. 'No, it isn't, Bo'sun. It's just that you're not square with the hole. Push it to the left a bit.'

The Bo'sun levered the crate with his foot. It

tilted suddenly, then fell with a splash into the water below.

Another rivet snapped.

'Quick!' the Second Mate said, his voice almost a whisper, as if he feared anything louder might decide the fate of the bulkhead which was the only protection for the men in Number One hold. 'More crates, as fast as you can!'

Tim turned, to find that Rory McGuinness and two of the crew were right behind him—in fact there was a queue of crates waiting to be dropped into the hole.

The splashing continued until thirty crates had been dropped, then became a dull thudding that showed they had now created an island of crates rising above the level of the water. No longer were the seas able to break in unimpeded and slam with the force of a gigantic steam hammer against the leaking bulkhead.

Some of the crew began to relax, but Rory McGuinness urged them on. 'Those crates won't stand up to the seas for long. We need more on top—right up to the level of the hole.'

Tim, Joe, and the Bo'sun moved out of the cramped space to let another team take its turn at the job of tipping the crates down the hole. They went back to Number One hatch, where the derricks were still bringing up further loads from the depths of the bottom hold. The men down there were working up to their waists in water, but still struggling to make up loads to shackle to the derricks. Water cascaded off each load as it rose up to the deck.

Tim looked up at the wing of the bridge, and waved to his father.

But Captain Allison wasn't looking. He was staring astern, at the lean grey bows of a corvette beginning to appear through the smoke!

11

Rory McGuinness came out of the forecastle and saw the corvette at the same time as Tim. He sprinted along the fore deck, waving Tim and Joe to join him. With no idea where he was going, they ran behind him, past the cabin block and the gaping ruin of the midships hatch. As he went, Rory waved more men to follow, and by the time he reached the ladder down to the well deck he had a dozen in all.

'Winches!' he shouted. 'Hoist the derricks. Get some of those big crates up on to the poop.'

Tim grabbed a winch handle, but was pushed away by the Bo'sun. 'Sorry, Tim, this needs experience. Stand by below to shackle up those crates.'

It was only when three crates were lined up on the poop that a glimmering of Rory's plan came to Tim. It was a wild gamble on the knowledge that some of the crates contained arms—and that there'd be hand grenades or mortar shells somewhere amongst them.

The corvette was now dead astern, a quarter of

a mile away and coming up fast through the murk. Old Screamer was starting to make thicker smoke again, but too late to do anything except upset the aim of the Mulanda gunners. Two shells in rapid succession hit the water within fifty yards of the ship. A signal lamp gleamed on the bridge of the corvette, flashing a morse code message that Jim was able to spell out. 'HEAVE TO, OR I SINK YOU.'

Rory McGuinness's answer was to wave six men to one of the crates on the poop. He knocked out the pins supporting the poop rail, then yelled, 'Heave!'

The crate shifted a few inches nearer the scuppers.

'Heave!'

Another few inches.

'All right, boys. This time does it. She's only a hundred yards astern.'

The crate teetered on the edge, then dropped. For a few seconds it vanished, then bobbed up to the surface midway between the two ships.

'Get ready with your next,' yelled Rory.

Tim, down in the well deck, leaned over the rail and watched the bows of the corvette race through the water towards the crate. For a moment it looked as though they would pass to starboard of it, then, just at the right moment, a cross sea carried the crate straight into the corvette's path. The bows of the speeding ship smashed into the crate, throwing up huge jagged splinters of wood.

But nothing else happened.

'Heave!' Rory McGuinness was yelling again.

Six men put their shoulders to the second crate. It balanced for a few seconds on the edge of the scuppers, then dropped into the wake from the propeller.

It took longer than the first to return to the surface, and when it did, only a small portion stuck up above the water. Tim watched, fascinated, as the corvette ploughed straight on towards it.

The force of the explosion threw him flat on the deck. Joe, at the top of the poop ladder, somersaulted backwards and landed on top of him with a weight that knocked all the breath out of him. A sheet of flame shot up high into the sky, followed immediately by more explosions as the corvette's boilers went up.

Old Screamer's steering engine rattled and clanked as the ship swung round in a tight circle to search the sea for survivors.

But it was a forlorn hope. There was not even floating wreckage. Rory McGuinness turned slowly away from the rail, where he had been peering